Among the fondest and most memorable moments of childhood are the discoveries of songbirds nesting in the backyard. The distinctive, mud-lined nests of robins and their beautiful blue eggs captivate people of all ages. Likewise, the nesting activities of house wrens, cardinals, chickadees and other common birds can stimulate a lifelong interest in nature.

Introduction

As you learn to enjoy the beauty of birdlife around their home, you may wish to improve the "habitat" in your yard so that more birds will visit your property. You can attract birds by placing bird feeders, nest boxes, and bird baths in your yard, and by planting a variety of trees, shrubs, and flowers. These can provide good nesting sites, winter shelter, places to hide from predators and natural food supplies that are available year-round.

Backyard bird feeding is a convenient way to enjoy wildlife. More than 65 million Americans of all ages watch, feed and landscape for birds.

It doesn't matter where you live—in an apartment, townhouse or single family dwelling, in the city, suburbs or country. Just stand still and you'll hear them: wild birds. It is hard to imagine life without them.

Bird watching is one of the fastest growing forms of outdoor recreation in the country. Each year millions of people discover for the first time the joys of birdwatching. It's easy to understand why. Birds are fun to watch.

And you can watch them just about everywhere. The most convenient place to start is right in your own backyard. All it takes to get their attention is food or water, a place to build a nest and appropriate vegetation.

photo:
Hollingsworth/USFWS

3

Backyard Bird Feeding

When you want to attract a particular bird species and keep it coming back to your backyard, what you do will be determined by where you live, and the time of year. For example, on any winter day, you are likely to see a cardinal at a sunflower feeder in Virginia, a goldfinch at a thistle feeder in Illinois and hummingbirds at a nectar feeder in southern California.

A bird field guide has pictures of different birds and will help you find the names for the birds you're likely to see and the time of year you're most likely to see them. So, first determine what birds are likely to occur in your area.

Feeder Selection

When the ground is covered with snow and ice, it's hard to resist just tossing seed out the door. But it's healthier for the birds to get their handouts at a feeding station, rather than off the ground. Regardless of the season, food that sits on the ground for even a short time is exposed to contamination by dampness, mold, bacteria, animal droppings, lawn fertilizers and pesticides.

You can start simply with a piece of scrap wood elevated a few inches above the ground. Add a few holes for drainage and you've built a platform feeder. It won't be long before the birds find it.

There are several factors to consider after you've decided to feed birds in your backyard.

Placement

Where do you want to watch your birds? From a kitchen window...a sliding glass door opening onto a deck...a second-story window?

Pick a location that is easy to get to. When the weather is bad and birds are most vulnerable, you may be reluctant to fill a feeder that is not in a convenient spot near a door or an accessible window. Also, pick a site where discarded seed shells and bird droppings won't be a cleanup problem.

Put your feeder where the squirrels can't reach. Squirrels become a problem when they take over a bird feeder, scaring the birds away and tossing seed all over. Squirrels have been known to chew right through plastic and wooden feeders.

If you've seen squirrels in your neighborhood, it is safe to assume they will visit your feeder. Think long and hard before you hang anything from a tree limb. Squirrels are incredibly agile, and any feeder hanging from a tree is likely to become a squirrel feeder.

In the long run, a squirrel-proof feeder or any feeder on a pole with a baffle is the least aggravating solution. The most effective squirrel-proof feeder is the pole-mounted metal "house" type.

Photo: Kevin Tennyson, USDOI

6

If you must hang a feeder, select a tube protected with metal mesh. Most plastic "squirrel-proof" feeders, despite manufacturers' claims, may eventually succumb to the squirrels. Any wood or plastic feeder can be effective when mounted on a pole with a plastic or metal baffle, if the pole is at least 10 feet or more from a tree limb or trunk (squirrels can jump great distances).

Durability

Bird feeders are made from a variety of materials. You can buy disposable plastic bag feeders; feeders made of cloth, nylon, vinyl and metal netting; clear, lexan, colored and PVC plastic tubes; ceramic and terra cotta; redwood, western cedar, birch, pine and plywood; sheet metal and aluminized steel; glass tubes and bottles.

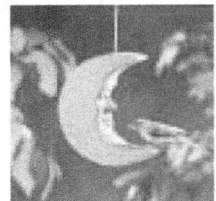

How long a feeder lasts depends on how well you maintain it, the effects of weather, and whether squirrels can get to it. Water can get into any feeder regardless of how carefully you protect it. Cloth, vinyl, nylon and metal netting feeders are inexpensive, but they do not protect your seed from spoiling in damp or wet weather. Improve them by adding a plastic dome.

Most wood, plastic, ceramic and solid metal feeders keep seed dry, but water can get into the feeding portals. Look for feeders with drainage holes in the bottoms of both the feeder hopper and the seed tray.

Even bowl-type feeders and trays with drainage holes will clog with seed and bird droppings that can mix with rainwater and be unhealthy for any animal. Look for shallow plate-like seed trays to catch dropped seeds while allowing spent seed shells to blow away.

When you feed birds, expect bird droppings and a leftover food mess. While you do not have to wash the feeder daily, you should clean it at least every few weeks. Diseases like salmonella can grow in moldy, wet seed and bird droppings in your feeder tray and on the ground below. Move your feeder a few feet each season to give the ground underneath time to assimilate the seed debris and bird droppings.

The maintenance required to keep your feeder clean varies according to the type of feeder. A thistle feeder for goldfinches should be cleaned about once a month depending on how often it rains. Feeding hummingbirds requires cleaning at the very least weekly, but preferably two or three times a week. Sunflower and suet feeders need to be cleaned only once a month.

Plastic, ceramic and glass feeders are easy to clean. Wash them in a bucket of hot, soapy water fortified with a capful or two of chlorine bleach. Use the same regimen with wood feeders, but substitute another disinfectant for the bleach so your wood won't fade.

Food Capacity

The ideal feeder capacity varies with your situation, and the types of birds you want to attract. If you feed hummingbirds, big feeders are not always better. One hummingbird will drink about twice its body weight (less than an ounce) a day. Early in the season, hummers are territorial and won't share a feeder. A sixteen-ounce feeder can be wasteful, or even lethal, because artificial nectar (sugar water) can ferment in the hot summer sun. A two-ounce feeder is more than enough for one hummer. Increase the size of your feeder depending on your location and how many hummers you see in your yard.

If you opt for a large-volume seed feeder, protect it from the weather and keep it clean. If after months of use, the birds suddenly abandon your feeder full of seed, it's time for a cleaning.

How Many Birds
If too many birds at your feeder become a problem, you can control their numbers by putting out smaller amounts of seed, or by using specialty seeds or restrictive feeders that will attract only certain species. If you fill your feeder only when it's empty, the birds will look for food elsewhere.

You can encourage small birds and discourage large birds with feeders that restrict access. Wood feeders with vertical bars and feeders covered with wire mesh frustrate larger birds.

The most non-selective feeders are the tray, platform or house feeders because they allow easy access by all birds.

Tube feeders without trays also restrict access to only small birds. Remove the perches, and you've further restricted the feeder to only those birds that can easily cling— finches, chickadees, titmice and woodpeckers.

If starlings are a problem at your suet feeder, discourage them by using a suet feeder with access only from the bottom. Starlings are reluctant to perch upside down. Chickadees and woodpeckers don't find that a problem.

You can virtually eliminate visits by birds you would rather not see by offering seeds they won't eat. If you use more than one type of seed, put them in separate feeders. This will reduce wasted seeds, as birds will toss unwanted seeds out of a feeder to get to their favorites.

Watch a feeder filled with a seed mix and you'll see the birds methodically drop or kick out most of the seeds to get to their favorite—sunflower.

Many birds prefer sunflower. Some prefer millet. A few prefer peanuts. Sparrows, blackbirds, doves and juncos will eat the other grains used in pre-made mixes: corn, milo, red millet, oats, wheat and canary seed. Birds will also kick out artificial "berry" pellets, processed seed flavored and colored to look like real fruit.

Black oil sunflower is the hands-down favorite of all the birds that visit tube and house feeders. Birds who visit platform feeders (doves and sparrows) favor white proso millet. Ducks, geese and quail will eat corn. Many cereal grains (corn, milo, oats, canary, wheat, rape, flax and buckwheat) in mixed bird seeds are NOT favorites of birds that visit tube feeders.

The most effective way to attract the largest variety of birds to your yard is to put out separate feeders for each food:

a starling-resistant suet feeder

a house feeder for sunflower

a bluebird feeder

a wire mesh cage feeder for peanut

a nectar feeder

a tube feeder for thistle

a stationary or tray fruit feeder

a house or platform feeder for millet

Suet Feeder

Thistle Feeder

Feeding Tray

Nut Feeder

Birds Attracted by Various Feeders and Foods

Tube Feeder with Black Oil Sunflower	goldfinches chickadees woodpeckers nuthatches	titmice redpolls pine siskins
...Adding a Tray to the Tube Feeder Will Also Attract	cardinals jays crossbills purple finches house finches	white-throated sparrows white-crowned sparrows
Tray or Platform Feeder—with Millet	doves house sparrows blackbirds juncos cowbirds towhees	white-throated sparrows tree sparrows white-crowned sparrows chipping sparrows
Tray or Platform Feeder—with Corn	starlings house sparrows grackles jays juncos bobwhite quail	doves ring-necked pheasants white-throated sparrows
Platform Feeder or Tube Feeder and Tray—with Peanuts	cardinals grackles titmice starlings jays	
Niger Thistle Feeder with Tray	goldfinches house finches purple finches redpolls pine siskins doves	chickadees song sparrows dark-eyed juncos white-throated sparrows
Nectar Feeder	hummingbirds orioles cardinals tanagers	woodpeckers finches thrushes

Fruit	orioles tanagers mockingbirds bluebirds thrashers cardinals woodpeckers	jays starlings thrushes cedar waxwings yellow-breasted chats
Hanging Suet Feeder	woodpeckers wrens chickadees nuthatches kinglets	thrashers creepers cardinals starlings
Peanut Butter Suet	woodpeckers goldfinches juncos cardinals thrushes	jays kinglets bluebirds wrens starlings
Hanging Peanut Feeder	woodpeckers chickadees titmice	

Uninvited Guests at the Birdfeeder

Once you get your bird feeding station up and running, you may run into problems with two kinds of uninvited guests—those interested in the seeds (squirrels and chipmunks, rats and mice, and starlings and house sparrows), and those interested in eating a bird for dinner (cats and hawks).

When a squirrel is at the feeder, you're not likely to see birds. Squirrels will scare off the birds while they eat the seed and sometimes they will eat the feeder too. The simplest solution is a squirrel-proof feeder or pole.

Starlings and house sparrows are not native to North America and are aggressive towards other species. Choose your feeder and seed to exclude these species if possible.

Chipmunks, rats and mice can also become a problem where there is seed spillage under the feeder. Don't use mixed bird seed, and if you don't have a squirrel problem, add a feeder tray.

Feral cats and your neighbor's tabby are a serious threat to many birds. Keep feeders away from brushpiles and shrubbery, as this offers cats the necessary cover to surprise birds.

If there are no cats in your neighborhood and you find a pile of feathers near your feeder, look for a full-bellied hawk perching on a tree nearby. Don't put out poisons or try to trap hawks though, as this is against state and federal law.

Questions about Feeding Wild Birds

When is the best time to start?

Usually, whenever the weather is severe, birds will appreciate a reliable supplemental food source. In northern areas, start before the onset of cold weather so birds have time to find the feeder.

When's the best time to stop?

Although you can feed birds year-round, especially with fruit and nectar, you can stop feeding seeds once a reliable supply of insects is available in the spring.

Is it best to stop feeding hummingbirds after Labor Day?

There is no evidence that feeding hummers after Labor Day will delay migration. Still, feeders in areas with sub-freezing winter weather should be removed shortly after that holiday. Tempting hummers to remain beyond normal departure dates is ill-advised.

How long does it take for birds to find a feeder?

It may take more time for birds to find window feeders than hanging or pole-mounted feeders. You may want to wrap aluminum foil around the top of the feeder hanger. Sometimes all it takes is the reflection of light on the foil to catch their attention.

My feeder is full of seeds. I haven't seen a bird in months. Am I doing something wrong?

When birds desert your feeder, it may be simply that a lot of natural food is available nearby. Or something may be wrong, such as spoiled seeds or a contaminated feeder. Throw the seeds away and wash the feeder. Look at where your feeder is placed. Be sure it's not vulnerable to predators. At the same time, make sure it is not in an open area, away from the cover in which birds usually travel.

Will birds' feet stick to metal feeders and perches in the wet winter weather?

Birds don't have sweat glands in their feet, so they won't freeze onto metal feeders. There's no need to cover any metal feeders parts with plastic or wood to protect birds' feet, tongues or eyes.

17

Do wild birds need grit?

Birds have no teeth to grind their food. The dirt, sand, pebbles and grit they eat sit in their crop and help grind up their food. Adding grit to your feeder is helpful, particularly in the winter and spring. Crushed eggshells do the same thing, and in the spring have an added benefit: they provide birds with extra calcium for producing eggs of their own.

Can birds choke on peanut butter?

There is no evidence that birds can choke on peanut butter. However, birds have no salivary glands. You can make it easier on them by mixing peanut butter with lard, cornmeal or grit. Your birds will appreciate drinking water too, from a bird bath or trough.

Won't suet go bad in the summer?

In the winter, raw beef fat from the local butcher is all you need for your suet feeder. When temperatures rise, raw fat can melt and get rancid. It's safer to use commercially rendered suet cakes in the spring and summer months. Rendering (boiling) the fat kills bacteria.

What is hummingbird nectar? Do hummers need nectar fortified with vitamins and minerals?

You can make your own hummingbird nectar by adding ¼ cup of sugar to a cup of boiling water. Remember, sugar water will ferment when left in the hot sun, turning nectar deadly. Do not put out a nectar feeder if you are not willing to clean it at least weekly, preferably twice a week.

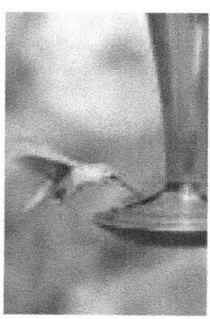

Hummers eat insects for their protein. There is no evidence that these tiny birds need vitamin and mineral supplements. There is also no evidence that adding red food coloring to nectar will harm the birds, but it probably is not necessary to attract them. Just put your feeder near red flowers or buy a red hummingbird feeder.

18

How can I avoid bees at my hummingbird feeder?

Bees will inevitably visit your hummingbird feeder, especially in hot weather. Little plastic bee guards may help keep them from getting nectar but it won't stop them from trying. Don't take the chance of contaminating your nectar by putting vegetable oil around the feeding portals. One solution is to add a few small feeders away from where people are likely to be bothered by bees.

How close to my window can I put a feeder?

Birds will come right to your window. Sometimes it takes a while for them to overcome their initial reluctance, so be patient. Don't worry that a feeder on the window will cause birds to fly into the window. Birds fly into the window because they see the reflection of the woods. Window feeders and decals help break up the reflection.

Is cracked corn coated with a red dye safe to use?

No. The red or pink coating is capstan, a fungicide used on seeds meant for planting. If you buy a bag of cracked corn or other seed treated with capstan, return it to the store. It can kill horses, other mammals and wild birds.

I bought a bag of sunflower seeds early in the spring. Over the summer I first noticed worms, then moths. What can I do to keep the bugs out?

Moths lay their eggs in sunflower seeds. The eggs lay dormant as long as the seeds are stored in a cool dry place. In the summer, seeds get hot and the eggs hatch. The best way to avoid this problem is to buy seeds in smaller quantities, or store your seeds in a cool, dry place. It also helps to know where your retailer stores the seed. An air-conditioned storage unit is the better choice.

Insects also lay their eggs in burlap bags. Don't buy seeds in burlap bags. Don't buy seed in paper and plastic bags with patched holes. That may be a sign of insect or rodent infestation.

Homes for Birds

Birds You Can
Attract to Nest
Boxes

Many of the birds that visit feeders
and baths may stay and nest in
nearby trees. Most of them, including
cardinals, doves and orioles, don't
nest in boxes. You can still help
them by considering their food and
shelter requirements in your
landscape plans.

More than two dozen North
American birds nest in bird houses.
The following descriptions will help
you determine which birds might
visit your neighborhood.

Bluebirds

If you put up a bluebird house near
an old field, orchard, park, cemetery
or golf course, you might have a
chance of attracting a pair of
bluebirds. They prefer nest boxes on
a tree stump or wooden fence post
between three and five feet high.
Bluebirds also nest in abandoned
woodpecker nest holes.

The most important measurement is
the hole diameter. An inch and a half
is small enough to deter starlings,
which, along with house sparrows,
have been known to kill bluebirds, as
well as adults sitting on the nest.
Bluebirds have problems with other
animals too. Discourage cats, snakes,
raccoons and chipmunks by mounting
the house on a metal pole, or use a
metal predator guard on a wood post.

American Robins

The robin is our largest thrush.
They prefer to build their nest in the
crotch of a tree. If you don't have an
appropriate tree, you can offer a
nesting platform. Pick a spot six
feet or higher up on a shaded tree
trunk or under the overhang of a
shed or porch. Creating a "mud
puddle" nearby offers further
enticement, as robins use mud to hold
their nests together.

20

Chickadees,
Nuthatches
and Titmice

Chickadees, titmice and nuthatches share the same food, feeders, and habitat. If you put a properly designed nest box in a wooded yard, at least one of these species might check it out.

Put chickadee houses at eye level. Hang them from limbs or secure them to tree trunks. The entrance hole should be $1\frac{1}{8}$ inches to attract chickadees, yet exclude house sparrows. Anchor houses for nuthatches on tree trunks five to six feet off the ground.

Brown Creepers
and
Prothonotary
Warblers

Look for brown creepers to nest behind the curved bark of tree trunks. In heavily wooded yards, slab bark houses appeal to creepers. Prothonotary warblers also prefer slab bark houses, or bluebird boxes attached to a tree trunk, but theirs must be placed over water (lakes, rivers or swamps) with a good canopy of trees overhead.

21

Wrens don't seem to be very picky about where they nest. Try nest boxes with a 1 inch x 2 inch horizontal slot (1½ inch x 2½ inch for the larger Carolina wrens) instead of a circle. These are easier for the wrens to use. However, the larger the opening, the more likely it is house sparrows will occupy the box.

Wrens are known for filling a nest cavity with twigs, regardless of whether they use the nest to raise their young. Since male house wrens build several nests for the female to choose from, hang several nest boxes at eye level on partly sunlit tree limbs. Wrens are sociable and will accept nest boxes quite close to your house.

Tree and Violet-green Swallows

Tree swallows prefer nest boxes attached to dead trees. Space the boxes about seven feet apart for these white-bellied birds with iridescent blue-green backs and wings. The ideal setting for these insect-eaters is on the edge of a large field near a lake, pond or river.

Violet-green swallows nest in forested mountains of the West; boxes placed on large trees in a semi-open woodland will attract them.

Barn Swallows and Phoebes

If you have the right habitat, like an open barn or old shed, barn swallows and phoebes are easy to attract. It's their nesting behavior, not their plumage or song, that catches your attention. However, these birds tend to nest where you would rather not have them: on a ledge right over your front door. To avoid a mess by your door, offer the birds a nesting shelf nearby where you'd rather have them.

Purple Martins Many people want martins in their yards because, it's been said, these birds eat 2,000 mosquitoes a day. While it's true that they eat flying insects, don't expect purple martins to eliminate mosquitoes in your yard completely. Martins prefer dragonflies, which prey on mosquito larvae. If you want to help rid your yard of mosquitoes, put up a bat roosting box. One bat can eat thousands of mosquitoes a night.

Martins are entertaining creatures, however, and you'll enjoy watching their antics in your backyard. You have the best chance of attracting martins if you put a house on the edge of a pond or river, surrounded by a field or lawn. Martins need a radius of about 40 feet of unobstructed flying space around their houses. A telephone wire nearby gives them a place to perch in sociable groups.

Martins nest in groups, so you'll need a house with a minimum of four large rooms—6 or more inches on all sides, with a 2 1/2 inch entrance hole about 1 1/2 inches above the floor. Ventilation and drainage are critical factors in martin house design. Porches, railings, porch dividers and supplemental roof perches, like a TV antenna, make any house more appealing.

You can also make houses from gourds by fashioning an entrance hole and small holes in the bottom for drainage. If you use gourds, it's not necessary to add railings and perches. Adult martins will perch on the wire used to hang the houses. Before you select a house, think about what kind of pole you're going to put it on. Martins occupy a house ten to twenty feet off the ground. Some poles are less cumbersome than others.

Gourd houses are the easiest to set up. String them from a wire between two poles, from a sectional aluminum pole, or on pulleys mounted to a crossbar high up on a pole.

You can mount lightweight aluminum houses for martins on telescoping poles, providing easy access for maintenance and inspection. Because of their weight (more than 30 pounds), wood houses should not be mounted on telescoping poles. You'll have to use a sturdy metal or a wood pole attached to a pivot post. The problem with this lowering technique is that you can't tilt the house without damaging the nests inside. If you put your house on a shorter, fixed pole, ten to twelve feet high, you can use a ladder to inspect and maintain it.

Flycatchers

The great crested flycatcher and its western cousin, the ash-throated flycatcher, are common in wooded suburbs and rural areas with woodlots. Their natural nesting sites are abandoned woodpecker holes. Flycatchers may nest in a bird house if it is placed about ten feet up in a tree in an orchard or at the edge of a field or stream. This is a longshot, but well worth the effort if you are successful.

Woodpeckers

You can attract all types of woodpeckers with a suet feeder, but only the flicker is likely to use a bird house. They prefer a box with roughened interior and a floor covered with a two-inch layer of wood chips or coarse sawdust. Flickers are especially attracted to nest boxes filled with sawdust, which they "excavate" to suit themselves. For best results, place the box high up on a tree trunk, exposed to direct sunlight.

Try building a birdhouse for the other species of woodpeckers following the guidelines in this booklet. You might be surprised!

Owls

Most owls seldom build their own nests. Great horned and long-eared owls prefer abandoned crow and hawk nests. Other owls (barred, barn, saw-whet, boreal and screech) nest in tree cavities and bird houses.

Barn owls are best known for selecting nesting sites near farms. Where trees are sparse, these birds will nest in church steeples, silos and barns. If you live near a farm or a golf course, try fastening a nest box for owls about 15 feet up on a tree trunk.

Screech owls prefer abandoned woodpecker holes at the edge of a field or neglected orchard. They will readily take to boxes lined with an inch or two of wood shavings. If you clean the box out in late spring after the young owls have fledged, you may attract a second tenant—a kestrel. Trees isolated from larger tracts of woods have less chance of squirrels taking over the box.

Selecting a House

In the bird house business, there's no such thing as "one size fits all." Decide which bird you want to attract, then get a house for that particular bird. Look through any book or catalog and you'll see bird houses of all sizes and shapes, with perches and without, made of materials you might not have thought of: recycled paper, gourds, plastic, rubber, pottery, metal and concrete. The proper combination of quality materials and design makes a good birdhouse.

photo: Bill French/
USFWS

Materials

Wood is just about the best building material for any birdhouse. It's durable, has good insulating qualities and breathes. Three-quarter-inch thick bald cypress and red cedar are recommended. Pine and exterior grade plywood will do, but they are not as durable.

It makes no difference whether the wood is slab, rough-cut or finished, as long as the inside has not been treated with stains or preservatives. Fumes from the chemicals could harm the birds.

There's no need to paint cypress and cedar, but pine and plywood houses will last longer with a coat of water-based exterior latex paint. White is the color for purple martin houses. Tan, gray or dull green works best for the other cavity nesting species. The dull, light colors reflect heat and are less conspicuous to predators. Don't paint the inside of the box or the entrance hole.

Regardless of which wood you select, gluing all the joints before you nail them will extend the life of your bird house. Galvanized or brass shank nails, hinges and screws resist rusting and hold boxes together more tightly as they age.

Resist the temptation to put a metal roof on your bird house. Reflective metal makes sense for martin houses up on a sixteen-foot pole, but when it's tacked onto the roof of a wood chickadee house, the shiny metal is more likely to attract predators.

Natural gourds make very attractive bird houses. They breathe, and because they sway in the wind they are less likely to be taken over by house sparrows and starlings.

Grow your own gourds and you'll have dozens to choose from in the years ahead. If you don't have the space to grow them, a coat of polyurethane or exterior latex (on the outside only) will add years to the one you have.

Properly designed pottery, aluminum (for purple martins only), concrete and plastic houses are durable, but don't drop them.

Be sure to provide ventilation, drainage, and easy access for maintenance and monitoring. Concrete (or a mix of concrete and sawdust) offers protection other houses cannot: squirrels can't chew their way in.

Design

How elaborate you make your bird house depends on your own tastes. In addition to where you place the box, the most important considerations are: box height, depth, floor dimensions, diameter of entrance hole and height of the hole above the box floor.

Refer to the following chart before building your nest box, keeping in mind that birds make their own choices, without regard for charts. So don't be surprised if you find tenants you never expected in a house you intended for someone else. Now that you have the correct dimensions for your bird house, take a look at how to make it safe: ventilation, drainage, susceptibly to predators, and ease of maintenance.

Nest Box Dimensions

Species	Floor size (inches)	Depth (top to bottom) (inches)
American Robin*	7x8	8
Eastern & Western Bluebirds	5x5	8–12
Mountain Bluebird	5x5	8–12
Chickadee	4x4	8–10
Titmouse	4x4	10–12
Ash-throated Flycatcher	6x6	8–12
Great Crested Flycatcher	6x6	8–12
Phoebe*	6x6	6
Brown-headed/ Pygmy/ Red-breasted Nuthatch	4x4	8–10
White-breasted Nuthatch	4x4	8–10
Prothonotary Warbler	5x5	6
Barn Swallow*	6x6	6
Purple Martin	6x6	6
Tree and Violet- Green Swallows	5x5	6–8

*Use nesting shelf, platform with three sides and an open front

Entrance Height above floor (inches)	Entrance Diameter (inches)	Height above ground (feet)
—	—	
6–10	$1^{1}/_{2}$	4–6
6–10	$1^{1}/_{2}$	4–6
6–8	$1^{1}/_{8}$	4–15
6–10	$1^{1}/_{4}$	5–15
6–10	$1^{1}/_{2}$	5–15
6–10	$1^{3}/_{4}$	5–15
—	—	8–12
6–8	$1^{1}/_{4}$	5–15
6–8	$1^{3}/_{8}$	5–15
4–5	$1^{1}/_{8}$	4–8
—	—	8–12
1–2	$2^{1}/_{4}$	6–20
4–6	$1^{1}/_{2}$	5–15

Species	Floor size (inches)	Depth (top to bottom) (inches)
Downy Woodpecker	4x4	8–10
Hairy Woodpecker	6x6	12–15
Lewis's Woodpecker	7x7	16–18
Northern Flicker	7x7	16–18
Pileated Woodpecker	8x8	16–24
Red–Headed Woodpecker	6x6	12–15
Yellow–bellied Sapsucker	5x5	12–15
Bewick's/ House Wrens	4x4	6–8
Carolina Wren	4x4	6–8
Barn Owl	10x18	15–18
Screech–Owl and Kestrel	8x8	12–15
Osprey	48x48 (platform)	
Red–tailed Hawk/Great Horned Owl	24x24 platform	
Wood Duck	10x18	10–24

*Use nesting shelf, platform with three sides and an open front

Entrance Height above floor (inches)	Entrance Diameter (inches)	Height above ground (feet)
6–8	$1\frac{1}{4}$	5–15
9–12	$1\frac{1}{2}$	8–20
14–16	$2\frac{1}{2}$	12–20
14–16	$2\frac{1}{2}$	6–20
12–20	3x4	15–25
9–12	2	10–20
9–12	$1\frac{1}{2}$	10–20
4–6	$1\frac{1}{4}$	5–10
4–6	$1\frac{1}{2}$	5–10
4	6	12–18
9–12	3	10–30
12–16	4	10–20

Ventilation   You should provide air vents in bird boxes. There are two ways to provide ventilation: leave gaps between the roof and sides of the box, or drill 1/4 inch holes just below the roof.

Drainage   Water becomes a problem when it sits in the bottom of a bird house. A roof with sufficient slope and overhang offers some protection. Drilling the entrance hole on an upward slant may also help keep the water out. Regardless of design, driving rain will get in through the entrance hole. You can assure proper drainage by cutting away the corners of the box floor and drilling 1/4-inch holes. Nest boxes will last longer if the floors are recessed about 1/4 inch.

Entrance Hole   Look for the entrance hole on the front panel near the top. A rough surface both inside and out makes it easier for the adults to get into the box and, when it's time, for the nestlings to climb out.

If your box is made of finished wood, add a couple of grooves outside below the hole. Open the front panel and add grooves, cleats or wire mesh to the inside. Never put up a bird house with a perch below the entrance hole. Perches offer starlings, house sparrows and other predators a convenient place to wait for lunch. Don't be tempted by duplexes or houses that have more than one entrance hole. Except for purple martins, cavity-nesting birds prefer not to share a house. While these condos look great in your yard, starlings and house sparrows are inclined to use them.

Bird houses should be easily accessible so you can see how your birds are doing and clean out the house. Monitor your bird houses every week and evict unwanted creatures such as house sparrows or starlings.

Be careful when you inspect your bird boxes—you may find something other than a bird inside. Don't be surprised to see squirrels, mice, snakes or insects. Look for fleas, flies, mites, larvae and lice in the bottom of the box. If you find insects and parasites, your first reaction may be to grab the nearest can of insect spray. If you do, use only insecticides known to be safe around birds: 1 percent rotenone powder or pyrethrin spray. If wasps are a problem, coat the inside top of the box with bar soap.

Here's how to check your nest boxes for unwanted visitors:

Watch the nest for 20–30 minutes. If you don't see or hear any birds near the box, go over and tap on the box. If you hear bird sounds, open the top and take a quick peek inside. If everything is all right, close the box. If you see problems (parasites or predators), remove them and close the box.

A bird house with easy access makes the job simple. Most bird houses can be opened from the top, the side, the front or the bottom. Boxes that open from the top and the front provide the easiest access. Opening the box from the top is less likely to disturb nesting birds. It's impossible to open a box from the bottom without the nest falling out. While side- and front-opening boxes are convenient for cleaning and monitoring, they have one drawback: the nestlings may jump out. If this happens, don't panic. Pick them up and put them back in the nest. Don't worry that the adults will reject the nestlings if you handle them. That's a myth; most birds have a terrible sense of smell.

If you clean out your nest boxes after each brood has fledged, several pairs may use the nest throughout the summer. Some cavity-nesting birds will not nest again in a box full of old nesting material.

In the fall, after you've cleaned out your nest box for the last time, you can put it in storage or leave it out. Gourds and pottery last longer if you take them in for the winter. You can leave your purple martin houses up, but plug the entrance holes to discourage starlings and house sparrows.

Leaving your wood and concrete houses out provides shelter for birds, flying squirrels and other animals during winter. Each spring, thoroughly clean all houses left out for the winter.

Proper box depth, and roof and entrance hole design will help reduce access by predators, such as raccoons, cats, opossums, and squirrels. Sometimes all it takes is an angled roof with a three-inch overhang to discourage small mammals.

The entrance hole is the only thing between a predator and a bird house full of nestlings. By itself, the $^3/_4$-inch wall is not wide enough to keep out the arm of a raccoon or house cat. Add a predator guard (a $^3/_4$-inch thick rectangular wood block with an entrance hole cut in it) to thicken the wall and you'll discourage sparrows, starlings, and cats.

Bird House Placement

Where you put your bird house is as important as its design and construction. Cavity-nesting birds are very particular about where they live. If you don't have the right habitat, the birds are not likely to find the house. You can modify your land to attract the birds you want to see by putting out a bird bath, planting fruit-bearing shrubs, including more trees or installing a pond with a waterfall.

Once you've matched up the right bird house with the appropriate habitat, you have to know where to put the nest box. Should you hang it from a tree limb, nail it to a fence or mount it on a pole or a tree trunk?

Most species require a fairly narrow range of heights for nest boxes. After checking the table in this brochure, pick a height that's convenient for you. After all, you will want to watch what goes on and keep the box clean. If you want to watch chickadees from your second floor window or deck, fifteen feet is reasonable but it's a lot easier to clean out a box at eye level.

Here are some tips on where to put bird houses:

don't put bird houses near bird feeders.

houses mounted on metal poles are less vulnerable to predators than houses nailed to tree trunks or hung from tree limbs.

use no more than four small nest boxes or one large box per acre for any one species.

put about 100 yards between bluebird boxes and 75 yards between swallow boxes. (If you have both species, pair the houses with one bluebird box 25 feet from a swallow box.)

don't put more than one box in a tree unless the tree is extremely large or the boxes are for different species.

if you have very hot summers, face the entrance holes of your boxes north or east to avoid overheating the box.

Protection from Predators

Cats

Nesting birds are extremely vulnerable to cats, as are fledglings and birds roosting for the night. Bell collars on cats offer birds little protection. Nailing a sheet metal guard or cone to a tree trunk is unsightly, but may deter less agile felines. Houses mounted on metal poles are the most difficult for predators to reach, especially if you smear the poles with a petroleum jelly and hot pepper mixture. The best deterrent is for owners to keep their cats inside whenever possible.

Dogs

Pet dogs are a hazard to nestlings in the spring and summer. Don't let your dog run loose during nesting time.

Squirrels

Red squirrels, and sometimes gray squirrels, can become a serious menace to bird houses and the birds themselves. If you find your nest hole enlarged, chances are a red squirrel is the culprit. Once inside the box, squirrels make a meal of the eggs and young. Adding a predator guard made of sheet metal to the entrance hole is usually enough to keep squirrels out.

Raccoons and Opossums

Raccoons and opossums will stick their arms inside nest boxes and try to pull out the adult, young, and eggs. Adding a $3/4$-inch thick predator guard to the bird house or an inverted cone to its pole support is a simple solution.

Snakes

Snakes play an important part in the balance of nature. If you find one in your bird house, don't kill it. Snake-proof your house by putting it on a metal pole lathered with petroleum jelly or red cayenne pepper.

39

House Sparrows and Starlings

If you don't discourage them, these two nuisance species introduced from Europe will harass or kill cavity-nesting birds. Since house sparrows and starlings are not protected by law, you may destroy their nests. But remember, other birds are protected by law.

House Wrens

House wrens sometimes interfere with the nesting success of other birds by puncturing their eggs. But, unlike the house sparrow and starling, these birds are native to North America and are protected by law. Don't be tempted to intervene when wrens appear at your backyard birdhouse.

Insects

Many insects lay their eggs and pupate in bird houses. Inspect your bird houses for signs of gypsy moths, blow flies, wasps, ants, gnats and bees. Keep bees and wasps from attaching their nests by coating the inside of the roof with bar soap. In areas where gypsy moths abound, avoid placing boxes in oak trees, which the gypsy moths favor.

Pyrethrin and rotenone insecticides are recommended for killing fly larvae, bird lice and mites after birds have finished nesting for the season.

Attracting Birds

As people learn to enjoy the beauty of birds around their home, they may wish to improve the "habitat" in their yard so that more birds will visit their property. You can attract birds by placing bird feeders, nest boxes and bird baths in your yard, and by planting a variety of trees, shrubs, and flowers. These can provide good nesting sites, winter shelter, places to hide from predators and natural food supplies that are available year-round.

Landscaping for Birds

The most surefire way to attract birds to your backyard is to make certain the appropriate habitat is available to them. You may be lucky and already have a good supply of food, shelter, and water available for our feathered friends. In that case, you have to do little more than stand back and watch.

However, for most backyards, bird habitat must be created. It's called "landscaping for birds" and it can be as simple or extravagant as you wish. Whatever the approach, anyone who has ever tried this type of landscaping comes away with a real love for it after their first sparkling hummingbirds hover at the coral bells, or the perky catbird comes down for a drink of water from the birdbath, or the sleek waxwings gather en masse to sample bittersweet berries.

Benefits of Landscaping for Birds

You can derive many benefits from landscaping to attract birds to your yard:

Increased Wildlife Populations

You can probably double the number of bird species using your property with a good landscaping plan.

Energy Conservation

By carefully arranging your conifer and hardwood trees, you can lower winter heating and summer cooling bills for your house.

Soil Conservation

Certain landscape plants can prevent soil erosion.

Natural Beauty

A good landscaping plan contributes to a beautiful, natural setting around your home that is pleasing to people as well as birds.

Wildlife Photography

Wildlife photography is a wonderful hobby for people of all ages.

Birdwatching

Try keeping a list of all the birds you see in your yard or from your yard. Some people have counted nearly 200 species of birds in their yard!

Natural Insect Control

Birds such as tree swallows, house wrens, brown thrashers and orioles eat a variety of insects.

Food Production	Some plants that attract wildlife are also appealing to humans. People and wildlife can share cherries, chokecherries, strawberries, and crabapples.
Property Value	A good landscaping plan can greatly increase the value of your property by adding natural beauty and an abundance of wildlife.
Habitat for Kids	Some of the best wildlife habitats are the best habitats for young people to discover the wonders of nature. A backyard bird habitat can stimulate young people to develop a lifelong interest in wildlife and conservation.

Basics of Landscaping for Birds
Landscaping for birds involves nine basic principles:

Food	Every bird species has its own unique food requirements that may change as the seasons change. Learn the food habits of the birds you wish to attract. Then plant the appropriate trees, shrubs, and flowers to provide the fruits, berries, seeds, acorns, nuts and nectar.
Water	You may be able to double the number of bird species in your yard by providing a source of water. A frog pond, water garden, or bird bath will get lots of bird use, especially if the water is dripping, splashing or moving.
Shelter	Birds need places where they can hide from predators and escape from severe weather. Trees (including dead ones), shrubs, tall grass and bird houses provide excellent shelter.
Diversity	The best landscaping plan is one that includes a variety of native plants. This helps attract the most bird species.

43

Four Seasons	Give birds food and shelter throughout the year by planting a variety of trees, shrubs and flowers that provide year-round benefits.
Arrangement	Properly arrange the different habitat components in your yard. Consider the effects of prevailing winds (and snow drifting) so your yard will be protected from harsh winter weather.
Protection	Birds should be protected from unnecessary mortality. When choosing the placement of bird feeders and nest boxes, consider their accessibility to predators. Picture windows can also be dangerous for birds, who fly directly at windows when they see the reflection of trees and shrubs. A network of parallel, vertical strings spaced 4 inches apart can be placed on the outside of windows to prevent this problem. Be cautious about the kinds of herbicides and pesticides used in your yard. Apply them only when necessary and strictly according to label instructions. In fact, try gardening and lawn care without using pesticides. Details can be found in gardening books at the library.
Hardiness Zones	When considering plants not native to your area, consult a plant hardiness zone map, found in most garden catalogues. Make sure the plants you want are rated for the winter hardiness zone classification of your area.
Soils and Topography	Consult your local garden center, university or county extension office to have your soil tested. Plant species are often adapted to certain types of soils. If you know what type of soil you have, you can identify the types of plants that will grow best in your yard.

Plants for Wild Birds

Seven types of plants are important as bird habitat:

Conifers

Conifers are evergreen trees and shrubs that include pines, spruces, firs, arborvitae, junipers, cedars, and yews. These plants are important as escape cover, winter shelter and summer nesting sites. Some also provide sap, fruits and seeds.

Grasses and Legumes

Grasses and legumes can provide cover for ground nesting birds—but only if the area is not mowed during the nesting season. Some grasses and legumes provide seeds as well. Native prairie grasses are becoming increasingly popular for landscaping purposes.

Nectar-producing Plants

Nectar-producing plants are very popular for attracting hummingbirds and orioles. Flowers with tubular red corollas are especially attractive to hummingbirds. Other trees, shrubs, vines and flowers also can provide nectar for hummingbirds.

Summer-fruiting Plants

This category includes plants that produce fruits or berries from May through August. In the summer these plants can attract brown thrashers, catbirds, robins, thrushes, waxwings, woodpeckers, orioles, cardinals, towhees and grosbeaks. Examples of summer-fruiting plants are various species of cherry, chokecherry, honeysuckle, raspberry, serviceberry, blackberry, blueberry, grape, mulberry, plum and elderberry.

Fall-fruiting Plants

This landscape component includes shrubs and vines whose fruits ripen in the fall. These foods are important both for migratory birds which build up fat reserves before migration and as a food source for nonmigratory species that need to enter the winter season in good physical condition. Fall-fruiting plants include dogwoods, mountain ash, winter-berries, cottoneasters and buffalo-berries.

Winter-fruiting Plants

Winter-fruiting plants are those whose fruits remain attached to the plants long after they first become ripe in the fall. Many are not palatable until they have frozen and thawed many times. Examples are glossy black chokecherry, Siberian and "red splendor" crabapple, snowberry, bittersweet, sumacs, American highbush cranberry, eastern and European wahoo, Virginia creeper, and Chinaberry.

Nut and Acorn Plants

These include oaks, hickories, buckeyes, chestnuts, butternuts, walnuts and hazels. A variety of birds, such as jays, woodpeckers and titmice, eat the meats of broken nuts and acorns These plants also contribute to good nesting habitat.

How to Get Started

Think of this project as landscaping for birds. Your goal will be to plant an assortment of trees, shrubs and flowers that will attract birds. If you plan carefully it can be inexpensive and fun for the whole family. The best way to get started is to follow these guidelines:

Set Your Priorities

Decide what types of birds you wish to attract, then build your plan around the needs of those species. Talk to friends and neighbors to find out what kinds of birds frequent your area. Attend a local bird club meeting and talk to local birdwatchers about how they have attracted birds to their yards.

Use Native Plants When Possible

Check with the botany department of a nearby college or university or with your state's natural heritage program for lists of trees, shrubs, and wildflowers native to your area. Use this list as a starting point for your landscape plan. These plants are naturally adapted to the climate of your area and are a good long-term investment. Many native plants are both beautiful for landscaping purposes and excellent for birds. If you include nonnative plant species in your plan, be sure they are not considered "invasive pests" by plant experts. Check out the bird books in your local library.

Draw a Map of Your Property

Draw a map of your property to scale using graph paper. Identify buildings, sidewalks, power lines, buried cables, fences, septic tank fields, trees, shrubs and patios. Consider how your plan relates to your neighbor's property—will the tree you plant shade out the neighbor's vegetable garden? Identify and map sunny or shady sites, low or wet sites, sandy sites, and native plants that will be left in place.

Also identify special views that you wish to enhance—areas for pets, benches, picnics, storage, playing, sledding, vegetable gardens and paths.

Get Your Soil Tested

Get your soil tested by your local garden center, county extension agent or soil conservation service. Find out what kinds of soil you have and then find out if your soils have nutrient or organic deficiencies that fertilization or addition of compost can correct. The soils you have will help determine the plants which can be included in your landscaping plan.

47

Review the Seven Plant Habitat Components	Review the seven plant components described previously. Which components are already present? Which ones are missing? Remember that you are trying to provide food and cover through all four seasons. Develop a list of plants that you think will provide the missing habitat components.
Talk to Resource Experts	Review this plant list with landscaping resource experts who can match your ideas with your soil types, soil drainage and the plants available through state or private nurseries. People at the nearby arboretum can help with your selections. At an arboretum you can also see what many plants look like. Talk with local bird clubs, the members of which probably are knowledgeable about landscaping for birds.
Develop Your Planting Plan	Sketch on your map the plants you wish to add. Draw trees to a scale that represents three-fourths of their mature width, and shrubs at their full mature width. This will help you calculate how many trees and shrubs you need. There is a tendency to include so many trees that eventually your yard will be mostly shaded. Be sure to leave open sunny sites where flowers and shrubs can thrive. Decide how much money you can spend and the time span of your project. Don't try to do too much at once. You might try a five-year development plan.
Implement Your Plan	Finally, go to it! Begin your plantings and include your entire family so they can all feel they are helping wildlife. Document your plantings on paper and by photographs. Try taking pictures of your yard from the same spots every year to document the growth of your plants.

Maintain Your Plan

Keep your new trees, shrubs and flowers adequately watered, and keep your planting areas weed-free by use of landscaping film and wood chips or shredded bark mulch. This avoids the use of herbicides for weed control. If problems develop with your plants, consult a local nursery, garden center or county extension agent.

And Finally...

Make sure to take the time to enjoy the wildlife that will eventually respond to your landscaping efforts.

Protecting Bird Habitat

Each year your state wildlife agency, private conservation groups, the U.S. Fish & Wildlife Service, other federal agencies, and many private landowners and business leaders work together to conserve and manage millions of acres of habitat—swamps, forests, ponds and grasslands. These habitats provide nesting habitat for songbirds and shorebirds, ducks and geese, hawks and owls.

You can make a difference in helping protect habitats for migratory birds by joining a national, regional or local wildlife or habitat conservation organization. Also, each year thousands of individuals throughout the western hemisphere celebrate International Migratory Bird Day (IMBD) through bird festivals, walks and counts. Held annually on the second Saturday in May, IMBD is the hallmark event of Partners in Flight, an international coalition of federal, state, local government and non-government agencies and organizations, industry, the academic community, and private individuals. Partners in Flight's mission is to reverse the declines of some migratory bird species and raise awareness of the important role that migratory birds play in our lives. Look for an IMBD event in your area. For more information about IMBD, Partners in Flight or migratory bird related issues, contact U.S. Fish and Wildlife Service, Division of Migratory Bird Management, 4401 North Fairfax Drive, Suite 634, Arlington, VA 22203 or visit http://birds.fws.gov.

Another way that you can help preserve a disappearing but valuable natural resource—wetlands—is by buying Federal Duck Stamps at your local post office. Money from sales of these stamps is used to protect wetlands. For more information, write U.S. Fish & Wildlife Service, Federal Duck Stamp Office, 1849 C Street, NW, Washington, DC 20240. http://duckstamps.fws.gov.

Books

Additional Resources
A large variety of books are available on attracting, housing, feeding, and gardening for birds. Check your local library, book store, or the Internet, for a selection of books on attracting birds to your yard.

Web Sites

There are many good on-line resources for bird enthusiasts. Below are a few useful web sites that discuss some of the more popular backyard birds; general information on bird feeding, housing, and gardening for birds; ways to keep birds safe from predators; and opportunities for you to become citizen scientists just by watching birds at your feeder.

WildBirds.com—feeding and attracting
http://www.wildbirds.com

Birding/Wild Birds—backyard birds, birdhouses and feeders
http://www.birding.about.com/hobbies/birding

Backyard Wildlife Habitats—National Wildlife Federation
http://www.nwf.org/habitats

Cats Indoors—American Birding Conservancy
http://www.abcbirds.org/cats/catsindoors.htm

North American Bluebird Society
http://www.nabluebirdsociety.org

Purple Martin Conservation Association
http://www.purplemartin.org

BirdSource—FeederWatch and Classroom FeederWatch
http://birdsource.org

National Bird-Feeding Society
http://www.birdfeeding.org/

Stokes Birds at Home/Birding—feeding, housing, and gardening
http://www.stokesbirdsathome.com/birding

Disclaimer

The U.S. Fish and Wildlife Service intends no endorsement and cannot guarantee the accuracy of information found on these web sites.

www.ingramcontent.com/pod-product-compliance
Lightning Source LLC
Chambersburg PA
CBHW070501290526
45790CB00003B/1049